TRACKING DOWN

TUDORS
AND
STUARTS

IN BRITAIN

TUDORS
AND
STUARTS
IN BRITAIN
MOIRA BUTTERFIELD

Tracking Down

W
FRANKLIN WATTS
LONDON · SYDNEY

First published in 2010 by Franklin Watts

Franklin Watts
338 Euston Road
London NW1 3BH

Franklin Watts Australia
Level 17/207 Kent Street
Sydney, NSW 2000

A CIP catalogue record for this book is available
from the British Library.

Dewey number: 941.05

ISBN 978 0 7496 9236 0

Printed in China

Franklin Watts is a division of Hachette Children's Books,
an Hachette UK company.

www.hachette.co.uk

Editor: Sarah Ridley
Design: John Christopher/White Design
Editor in Chief: John C. Miles
Art director: Jonathan Hair
Picture research: Diana Morris

Picture credits:
Timothy Ball/istockphoto: 10. Caerphilly County Borough Council: 26, 27t. Carolyn Clarke/Alamy: 28. David
Dixon/NTPL: 19b. Fastfoto PL/PA /Topham: 20b. Steve Geer/istockphoto: 12. The Granger Collection/Topfoto: 8.
Chris Harvey/Shutterstock: 14t. Interfoto/Alamy: 6. Michael Jones/Alamy: front cover, 3. Lebrecht Music & Arts
PL/Alamy: 24. Nadia Mackenzie/NTPL: 18. The Mary Rose Trust: 17b. Bob Masters/Alamy: 29t. John C. Miles: 7.
K Miragaya/istockphoto: 14b. Museum of London: 9b, 23b. Justin Kasez Ninez/Alamy: 25t. Graham Oliver/Alamy:
25b, 30. pdtne/istockphoto: 13. Collection of the Earl of Pembroke, Wilton House, Wilts/Bridgeman PL: 27b.
Lara Platman: 23t. Private Collection/Bridgeman PL: 19t. Joel W Rogers/Corbis: 9t.
Science Museum/Science & Society PL: 29b. Suzib_100/Shutterstock: 11. The Times/Rex Features: 21.
Travel shots/Alamy: 17t. Eileen Tweedy/ Magdalene College Cambridge/Art Archive: 16.
Claudio Vizia/istockphoto: 20t. The Weald and Downland Open Air Museum: 22.

CONTENTS

THE TUDORS AND STUARTS

The Tudors and Stuarts were families who ruled England, Wales and eventually Scotland from 1485 to 1714. During this time huge changes occurred in the way the country was governed and how people lived their daily lives.

Turbulent Tudors

The Tudor Age began in 1485 when Henry Tudor defeated Richard III at the Battle of Bosworth, took the crown and became Henry VII. His son and three grandchildren ruled until 1603 when the last member of the family, Elizabeth I, died childless. Religion was a central part of life in those days, and in Tudor times there was great religious upheaval between Catholics and Protestants, leading to rebellion and invasion threats. You can discover stories from these troubled times by visiting the ruins of monasteries, pulled down on Tudor orders, or by exploring some of the grand houses built by Tudor nobles around the country. In some areas you can see a number of surviving Tudor buildings.

← Henry VII was an able king and a good administrator who put the finances of England, Wales and Ireland on a solid footing.

→ An engraved portrait of Stuart King Charles II. He became king at the restoration of the monarchy in 1660 after years of bloody fighting during the Civil Wars.

A monarch is lost

The Stuart dynasty began when James Stuart was crowned James I of England in 1603. He was a cousin of the Tudors and was already King of Scotland. The reign of the Stuarts was interrupted when the country was divided by civil war and James's son, Charles I, was beheaded by order of Parliament in 1649. The country had no monarch until 1660 when Charles II was invited back from exile abroad to claim the throne. Today you can visit Civil War battle sites and also the historic homes of people caught up in the fighting.

More people, more buildings

The Stuart era ended with the death of Queen Anne in 1714. By that time the population of the country had increased and cities and towns had grown across Britain. Buildings that have survived from these times range from grand royal palaces and cathedrals to manor houses, town houses and village homes. You may be able to find a Tudor or Stuart building somewhere near your home, and treasures from the time will be on display in local museums.

During Tudor and Stuart times major changes in politics, religion and world exploration had a big effect on everybody, from the super-wealthy to the very poor.

➜ A Puritan family, depicted in an engraving from the 1560s. Frivolity was frowned upon in the lives of 'the godly', as they called themselves.

Who's in charge?

Tudor monarchs had a court of nobles and top advisors around them to carry out their plans, and they could order anyone's imprisonment and execution if they wished. After the Civil War, when there was no monarch, Parliament was in charge. It was dominated by Puritans; people who believed in a hardline religious code and passed strict laws banning dancing, theatres and sport. They even tried to ban Christmas. On the return of King Charles II these laws were relaxed, but by now the monarchy had lost many of its powers to Parliament. From then on, the monarch and Parliament had to work together to govern, sometimes with great difficulty.

Money in the middle

In early Tudor times the monarch and nobles were by far the richest people in the country. Gradually, however, the middle classes began to share in the country's wealth. Merchants, traders and prosperous farmers made fortunes, built themselves fine houses and began to take part in government. Many made money by trading with lands abroad. New areas of the world, such as America, were discovered and opened up to trade, while ship design improved, enabling longer voyages.

↑ A replica of Sir Francis Drake's *Golden Hind*. The original sailed around the world between 1577 and 1580.

LOOK FOR

Tudor and Stuart treasures

Look out for Tudor and Stuart artefacts in museums and for buildings open to the public.

Everyday objects
Clothing, household items and even children's toys have survived, giving us glimpses of daily life.

Weapons and armour
These were warlike times, so weaponry and armour were needed.

Documents and paintings
Surviving documents give us a record of Tudor and Stuart life. Paintings provide evidence of what people looked like.

The poorest in the land

The poor lived as best they could by working on the land or as servants for other people. Those who could not work ran the risk of being thrown out of their homes or even being sent to prison, and many died from starvation or disease. In fact, life expectancy for everyone was much lower than it is today because there was very little effective medical treatment. Epidemics spread quickly and in the summer of 1665, during the reign of Charles II, a quarter of all the people in London died of the Plague, a disease spread by fleas that lived on the city's rat population.

← This onyx cameo portrait of Queen Elizabeth I, made in the 1500s, gives a good idea of what she looked like.

A ROYAL PALACE

The Tudor and Stuart monarchs had several fine palaces around London and they moved their court regularly between different buildings. Some of these palaces have long since disappeared but one of the grandest, Hampton Court, still survives today.

↑ The gatehouse and main Tudor frontage of Hampton Court Palace.

Fit for a king

Hampton Court Palace was originally built in the 1520s by Cardinal Wolsey, who was once Henry VIII's chief minister. Henry did not like his advisor living in a building grander than any of his own properties and he forced Wolsey to give him Hampton Court as a gift. Hampton Court gave Henry the chance to display his grandeur and power. In 1546 he entertained the French ambassador and 200 of his followers, as well as 1,300 members of his own court, for six whole days. The huge palace kitchens provided lavish banquets, and gold and velvet tents were set up in the palace grounds for the occasion.

Pleasure palace

Henry spent the equivalent of about £18 million adding luxuries to Hampton Court. He had bowling alleys, tennis courts and even a jousting yard built for the court's entertainment. The royal family had their own private suite, while the courtiers lived in rooms around an outer courtyard. Henry installed the latest inventions, including a magnificent new clock (see below), and toilets with running water. He had a lavatory block built, called the Great House of Easement, that could seat 28 people at a time.

▼ Henry VIII ordered that this clock be built at Hampton Court Palace.

GO VISIT

Hampton Court Palace

Among the attractions at Hampton Court Palace are the Tudor kitchens, the Chapel Royal where monarchs prayed and the Great Hall where they feasted. One of Henry VIII's six wives, Catherine Howard, was taken from Hampton Court to be imprisoned in the Tower of London (see pages 14–15), before being beheaded. She is said to haunt the palace, screaming!

Monarchs come and go

After Henry's reign, other Tudor and Stuart monarchs stayed at Hampton Court. For instance, James I held lots of riotous drunken parties there, with entertainment provided by William Shakespeare (see page 20). During the late Stuart era half the Tudor palace was knocked down and rebuilt in a grand new building style called baroque (see page 29). New gardens were laid out, including a giant maze which has since become world-famous. You can see both the Tudor and Stuart parts of the building along with portraits of some of its inhabitants, including Henry VIII, his six wives and his children.

REFORMATION RUINS

In 1536 Henry VIII ordered the destruction of monasteries across the land. Fountains Abbey in Yorkshire was the largest monastery to be shut, and its ruins can still be seen today.

Dissolution days

The destruction of the monasteries is called the 'Dissolution', and it happened because Henry VIII decided to divorce his first wife, Katherine of Aragon, in order to marry Anne Boleyn. When the Pope, who was head of the Catholic Church, refused to grant the divorce Henry declared himself head of the Church in England so that he could divorce without the Pope's permission. The monasteries were Catholic, and Henry wanted them destroyed so they would not challenge his power. He wanted their wealth, too. Many of them had valuable treasures and huge estates. The monks and nuns were turned out of their homes and given pensions to live on, but any who resisted were executed. In the years between 1520–1560, the Catholic Church lost power to Protestantism across Britain and parts of Europe, in an era called the 'Reformation'.

← The ruins of Fountains Abbey, Yorkshire. When it was shut, its lands were sold off, along with some of the building's stone.

Ways of the white monks

There were several types of monk in England, following different sets of religious rules. Fountains Abbey was the home of Cistercian monks, who followed a very strict life of prayer. Their pale wool gowns gave them the nickname 'the white monks'. The Abbey also had lay brothers, who had a less strict daily routine and did all the work needed to run the monastery and its farm.

Trouble in the north

Some were happy to see the end of Church power, but others found the changes hard to stomach. In Yorkshire there was an uprising called the Pilgrimage of Grace, and an army of over 30,000 men gathered to resist the King. Henry offered to listen to them and give them a general pardon. They accepted his promise but, once the rebel army disbanded, he went back on his word and had the leaders of the uprising hanged.

↑ The cellarium at Fountains Abbey. Amazingly, this has survived intact. The lay brothers ate, slept and socialised here.

Fountains Abbey

Fountains Abbey is now a World Heritage Site, and you can wander amongst its ruins in the footsteps of the white monks. You can see where they ate, slept and prayed, and visit a nearby mill where the lay brothers would have worked grinding crops from the Abbey farmland. As well as Fountains Abbey there are many other monastery ruins, both large and small, to visit around the country.

A DANGEROUS TOWER

During the rule of the Tudors and Stuarts there were many plots by other nobles to steal the throne. Those judged enemies of the monarch were imprisoned in the Tower of London, and sometimes tortured and executed there.

⬇ The Traitor's Gate entrance to the Tower of London (see text right).

Taken to the Tower

After the Tower was first founded in the 1080s, generations of monarchs, including the Tudors and Stuarts, used it as an impregnable prison for their most dangerous enemies. Prisoners were usually taken to the Tower by boat, often at night to avoid any attention. They were rowed into the Tower through a river entrance called Traitor's Gate. Inside they could look forward to long imprisonment and, in some cases, torture and execution. The highest-ranking prisoners were beheaded on Tower Green, within the tower walls and well away from any crowds who might support them.

⬇ The Tower of London stands on the River Thames, in the heart of the City.

Wrong religion

The Tower was a prison for traitors; people who were accused of threatening the security of the country. The strife began with Henry VIII's rejection of the leadership of the Catholic Pope (see page 12). His son Edward VI was a strong Protestant, but his daughter Mary I was a strong Catholic. His daughter Elizabeth I was a Protestant. So, over the years the Tower was home to many 'traitors' of both religions. Princess Elizabeth herself was imprisoned in the Tower for a few weeks during the reign of her sister Mary.

GO VISIT

The Tower of London

As well as being a traitor's prison, the Tower of London has been used as a zoo, a mint, an armoury and even an observatory. The Crown Jewels are on display there, guarded by the Yeoman Warders (nicknamed the 'Beefeaters'). Visitors can see Henry VIII's armour, learn the stories of the Tower prisoners and see Tower Green, the site of many notorious executions, including that of Henry VIII's wives Anne Boleyn and Catherine Howard.

Terrible tortures

Confessions were forced from some of the Tower's prisoners using torture. The most notorious torture instrument was the rack, which stretched a prisoner's body until the joints were dislocated and finally torn apart. Prisoners were also hung by manacles (thick iron cuffs) from the walls of their cells. Once found guilty, nobles faced beheading and religious heretics – those who disagreed with the monarch's choice of faith – were tied to a wooden stake and burnt alive in the streets of London.

⬆ One of Henry VIII's suits of armour can be seen at the Tower of London.

DISASTER AT SEA

Throughout Tudor and Stuart times there were threats of invasion from other European powers, and so England had to build up its armies and navy to defend itself. Henry VIII had new warships built for the navy, and the most famous example is the *Mary Rose*, not because it was successful in battle but because it sank before his eyes.

➤ A manuscript painting of Henry VIII's warship, the *Mary Rose*.

Added armoury

Henry VIII had lots of new warships built and for the first time they were armed with heavy cannons to fire at enemy ships. Prior to this new development, ships had only been used to transport soldiers or as floating platforms for hand-to-hand fighting. The *Mary Rose* had 91 guns and was one of the first ever craft able to fire a broadside; the name given to the tactic of firing all the guns on one side of the ship together. Her crew of about 500 men included sailors, soldiers and gunners. She was a type of ship called a carrack, built-up at the bow (front) into a high forecastle and made flat across the stern (back).

Disastrous day

In 1545 Henry VIII was watching from the shore when his fleet engaged a French invasion fleet in the Solent near Portsmouth. The *Mary Rose* fired a broadside at the enemy and began to turn, perhaps too sharply. She keeled over; water rushed in through the open gunports and she quickly capsized and sank. Few sailors could swim, so most of the crew drowned. Many of the crew were trapped onboard by netting draped over the rigging to stop enemy troops boarding. Although the French fleet were defeated, the sinking was a terrible loss, witnessed by the King.

▲ The hull of the *Mary Rose* is kept under special conditions, to stop it from falling apart.

GO VISIT

The *Mary Rose* and Tudor forts

Once it was raised from the seabed, the hull of the *Mary Rose* was put on display at the Portsmouth Historic Dockyard. The museum on site displays a wide variety of artefacts from the wreck, including a fascinating medicine chest that belonged to the ship's doctor. You can also visit Henry VIII's coastal fortresses at Deal in Kent, and at St. Mawes and Pendennis in Cornwall.

The *Mary Rose* returns

The wreck of the *Mary Rose* was rediscovered in the 1960s, and the remains of the hull were brought up to the surface in 1982 inside a specially-built steel cradle lined with airbags. As well as the ship timbers, the remains of around 200 crewmen were found along with 13,000 objects from onboard the wreck. They included furniture and lots of personal belongings. There were shoes, dice games, coins and even the remains of a rare musical woodwind instrument called a shawm.

◀ This perfectly preserved wooden pepper mill was recovered from the *Mary Rose*.

17

A GRAND HOUSE

Henry VIII's daughter Elizabeth I was the longest reigning Tudor monarch. During her 45-year rule – called the Elizabethan era – the country grew more prosperous, and grand manor houses were built around the country by nobles and court advisors. Montacute House in Somerset is a typical example.

Wealthy housebuilder

Elizabeth I's advisors were crucial to the smooth running of her kingdom. One of them was Sir Edward Phelips, who made his money as a prominent lawyer and used his fortune to build Montacute House in 1601, towards the end of the Queen's reign. Under her successor, James I, Sir Edward prosecuted Guy Fawkes, who famously tried to blow up the Houses of Parliament. However, the Phelips family fell out of royal favour when Sir Edward's son upset the King and was imprisoned in the Tower of London.

↓ Completed in 1601, Montacute House in Somerset was built to impress.

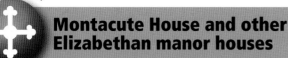

Montacute House and other Elizabethan manor houses

At Montacute House you can see a big collection of portraits of people from Tudor and Stuart times, and you can even sit eating an ice cream in one of the pudding houses, like one of Sir Edward Phelips's guests. There are lots of other Elizabethan manors around the country, both large and small, each with its own stories and treasures on show. Some played host to Elizabeth I herself, as she and her court often stayed as guests of her most prominent nobles.

➤ This fine portrait of Elizabeth I is at Montacute House.

Luxury Elizabethan-style

Like many Elizabethan manors Montacute was built in the latest style, with innovations such as mullioned glass windows (window panes divided up into sections) and a set of statues of historical heroes mounted on the walls. Inside there was a Grand Hall, kitchens, dining rooms and bedrooms, and a long gallery that was used for indoor exercise. The Phelips family decorated their new home with patterned plasterwork and wood panelling, and hung the very best luxury tapestries on the walls.

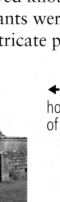

Elizabethan gardens

At the courts of both Elizabeth I and James I there were lots of parties and entertainments, often held outside in grand gardens. Although the Elizabethan garden no longer exists at Montacute, there are two surviving stone pavilions called 'pudding houses', where guests would come after dinner to eat their dessert and look out on the garden view. The Elizabethans loved knot gardens, where plants were laid out in intricate patterns.

◄ One of the pudding houses in the grounds of Montacute House.

A TRIP TO THE THEATRE

Theatre developed in Britain during the Elizabethan era and the Jacobean era (the name given to the reign of James I). William Shakespeare served both monarchs and his plays were performed at the royal court and at London theatres such as The Globe, now rebuilt near its original site.

The first theatres

England's first theatres were built during the reign of Elizabeth I, who loved plays and encouraged performances. Groups of actors – called companies – ran the theatres, but only with permission from royal officials. Many thought that theatres were scandalous places and tried to get them closed. Theatres were banned after the Civil Wars in the 1640s (see pages 24–25), but opened again when Charles II came to the throne in 1660.

↑ An engraving of William Shakespeare.

→ The Globe, a reconstruction of the original theatre, photographed from the air. It is close to the River Thames in London.

Inside The Globe

The modern reconstruction of The Globe is based on drawings and descriptions which show the original theatre as a round building, partly open to the sky, with the stage jutting out into the centre. The cheapest tickets were for the 'pit', the area around the stage, where the crowd moved around noisily and sometimes even heckled the actors. Wealthier people sat in balcony seats but the most important nobles may have sat in the 'Lord's Room', a private VIP balcony above the back of the stage.

↑ The Globe, London. Theatre-goers can stand to watch Shakespeare's plays from the pit, just like an Elizabethan audience.

GO VISIT

Shakespeare's Globe

In the summer months plays are performed at the authentic replica of Shakespeare's Globe, and all year-round there is a museum of Globe history on the site. You can also visit Shakespeare's birthplace, Stratford-upon-Avon, in Warwickshire. His wife Anne Hathaway's house is open to the public. Shakespeare's original play manuscripts are lost, but play copies made during his lifetime are kept at the British Library in London, and you can see them online.

Shakespeare's London

London was a crowded, stinking but lively capital, rapidly growing in size. Entertainments, such as theatres and taverns, were banned in the City area and they were only allowed on the south bank of the River Thames, where they lined a road called Bankside. Visitors paid a penny to come over the river by ferry. As well as plays, the theatres held cockfight shows and alongside the theatres there were bear-baiting pits, where crowds gambled on fights to the death between dogs and tethered bears. At this time, it was just a short walk from The Globe into fields and, in fact, most of what we now call London was farmland.

A BUSY KITCHEN

In Tudor and Stuart times noble families and the middle-classes had servants to run their homes. Cooks prepared meals in kitchens similar to the one at the Weald and Downland Open Air Museum.

➜ A modern cook at work in the reconstructed Tudor kitchen at the Weald and Downland Open Air Museum.

A farmhouse kitchen

The Winkhurst Tudor Kitchen is just one of 50 buildings at the Weald and Downland Open Air Museum. It was originally built in the 1540s, away from the main farmhouse it served in case of fire. It is made with wattle and daub; a wooden frame in-filled with woven sticks packed with mud and dung. The cook (usually a woman) had to keep the kitchen fire burning all day long, so it was very important for her to have enough firewood. She might have had three or four servants to help her, collecting wood and helping her cook meals for the farmer and his workers. Pots and pans and cooking utensils hung around her kitchen walls. The cook probably washed up her pots with ground-up eggshells.

Eating in the past

In Tudor times diners began to use plates for the first time, made of wood or pewter. They ate with knives and their fingers, which they washed in bowls of water set on the table. Meals would include seasonal vegetables and fruit from the garden or the hedgerows, along with local meat such as chicken, pork and wild rabbit. Wild birds such as blackbirds, doves and larks were added to the menu, too. The cook at Winkhurst would have smoked and salted meat and fish to preserve it for the winter, and she would have made her own cheese, bread and beer. Cooks flavoured the food with herbs and a few expensive spices imported from abroad.

↑ Poorer Tudor people ate a lot with their hands, as forks had not been introduced, and spoons were expensive.

Menus for rich and poor

→ Wealthy people served salt from elaborate silver salt cellars, such as this one.

Noble households had big kitchens with lots of staff, able to cook lavish banquets. Grand kitchens would have been very warm places to work, with several fires burning all the time. The rich looked down on vegetables as being food only fit for the poor, so they ate a lot of meat dishes. Meanwhile the poorest in Tudor society existed on pottage, a vegetable stew thickened with oats or barley.

GO VISIT

Weald and Downland Open Air Museum

Winkhurst Tudor Kitchen is part of the Weald and Downland Open Air Museum in West Sussex. A real-life cook works in the kitchen preparing Tudor meals, which you can sample when you visit. There are much grander kitchens at Hampton Court (see pages 10–11), and at Cowdray Castle in West Sussex, where the Earls of Southampton once entertained Henry VIII and Elizabeth I.

THE CROWN IS LOST

James I's son, Charles, became king in 1625, but civil war broke out during his reign and he became the only British monarch ever to be executed.

Clashing with the King

In Tudor times the monarch was seen as all-powerful, but by Charles I's day the English Parliament was beginning to disagree. Charles clashed with them over religion and over the taxes he wanted to impose on the country. He believed that, as monarch, he had a divine right sanctioned by God to do whatever he wished. When Parliament refused his money demands he shut the Parliament building. Eventually he had it reopened, but the angry Parliamentarians, led by Oliver Cromwell, refused him funding unless he agreed to their demands for more power. The King gathered an army and the Parliamentarians did the same, resulting in the English Civil War.

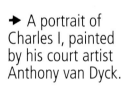

➔ A portrait of Charles I, painted by his court artist Anthony van Dyck.

GO VISIT

Naseby and other battle sites

You can visit the battlefield at Naseby, near Northampton, one of the most important battle sites in British history. There you can learn some of the facts about the Battle of Naseby, when Charles I's main army was defeated. There are other English Civil War battlefields around the country, and in the summer months battles are often re-enacted by Civil War societies.

▲ Members of an English Civil War society re-enact a battle.

The decisive battle

There were many battles and sieges around the country from 1642, but the turning point came on 14 June 1645, when the Parliamentarian New Model Army met the Royalist Army at Naseby. The armies were a mixture of cavalry (soldiers on horseback) and infantry (foot soldiers). Both sides had cannons, but after the battle most of the Royalist cannons were captured by the Parliamentarians. The Royalists were shattered and the King fled with his surviving troops, many of whom were tracked down and killed or imprisoned.

➡ The monument at Naseby which marks the site of the Civil War battle.

The aftermath of Naseby

Defeat for Charles I at Naseby led eventually to his trial and execution in 1649. It was an extraordinary change in British history. Suddenly there was no longer a monarch and Parliament was in charge. Oliver Cromwell became the 'Lord Protector' of the country and, temporarily, the Stuart line ended. The Parliamentarians are sometimes referred to as 'roundheads', but this was an insulting nickname they wouldn't have used themselves. It probably comes from their close-cropped haircuts, different from the fashionably-flowing locks of the 'cavaliers', the cavalry of the Royalist forces.

After the Battle of Naseby Charles I fled to Wales, where he visited Llancaiach Fawr Manor near Caerphilly. The manor has been preserved just as it was in 1645, and it is run as a living history museum, staffed by re-enactors who dress as people of the time.

➜ Re-enactors dressed as Stuart personalities, including King Charles I (centre), take part in living history days at Llancaiach Fawr Manor.

A failed visit

The manor was built in 1530, and it was partly fortified in case it was ever attacked. By the time the English Civil War broke out it was the home of the Prichard family. At first Edward Prichard raised money and men for the Royalists. However, after Charles I visited him in 1645, to gather more troops, Prichard changed sides and fought for the Parliamentarians. Many of Charles I's supporters became disillusioned with him, and, like Prichard, ended up on the winning side. Nobles who continued to support Charles lost their homes and lands at the end of the war.

Life goes on

Ordinary people had to try to carry on their lives as normal during the Civil War, but it would have been difficult. Family members sometimes disagreed with each other and occasionally fought on opposite sides. Edward Prichard's servants would have kept quiet about their own beliefs in order to safeguard their jobs. The Prichards had a large staff to run the house and farm estate. There were personal servants for family members, cooks and maids, as well as dairymaids, grooms and farm workers.

Civil War re-enactors at ♠
Llancaiach Fawr Manor
fire their muskets.

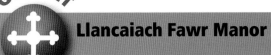

GO VISIT

Llancaiach Fawr Manor

At Llancaiach Fawr Manor visitors get the chance to see people working just as they did in 1645, and the re-enactors will answer questions about life in Stuart times. At Little Woodham in Hampshire you can visit another Stuart living history museum, this time a working village set in 1642. About 80% of people still lived in rural settlements such as Little Woodham in the 17th century, and even city dwellers were never far from the countryside.

Growing up in Stuart times

Many children died at a young age in both Tudor and Stuart times, as disease was rife. The Prichards' sons died in childhood, and only two daughters survived to adulthood. Wealthy families often had lots of children, in the hope that at least a few would survive. Only children of the rich were taught to read and write. Poor children were apprenticed to a trade or became farm labourers.

← A portrait of Charles I's children. Royal and noble children wore clothes made from the finest fabrics.

A MONARCH'S CATHEDRAL

Charles II was invited to return from exile to be crowned King in 1660, a date known as the 'Restoration'. He and his Stuart relatives reigned until 1714. This was a period when cities grew, especially London. Its skyline was changed forever by new buildings, including the magnificent Saint Paul's Cathedral.

Fire brings space

London was a crowded hotchpotch of narrow lanes and old wooden buildings, and when a baker's shop caught fire in 1666, fire spread easily from house to house. The Great Fire of London raged for four days, leaving the old City area gutted. Charles II commissioned the architect Sir Christopher Wren to plan a new London, and he rebuilt many churches, including Saint Paul's. The new structures were constructed from stone, not wood, and so the capital began to look very different from earlier times. The new building techniques and styles that Wren introduced soon appeared in other parts of the country, too.

← St Paul's Cathedral, London. Completed in 1708, St Paul's is Wren's best-known creation.

GO VISIT

St Paul's Cathedral and Stuart London

Saint Paul's Cathedral is in the oldest area of London, called the City. From nearby you could take a boat along the Thames to Greenwich, just as people did in Stuart times. Here you can visit the Royal Observatory, founded in 1675. The Old Royal Naval College complex was built by Wren in the 1690s as a home for retired or injured sailors.

← This reflecting telescope from the 1600s is in the collection of the Royal Observatory at Greenwich.

↑ People worship beneath the dome of St Paul's Cathedral, one of the biggest cathedral domes in the world.

New buildings, new ideas

Not everyone was convinced by Wren's radical plans, and he had to do a number of different designs before he was allowed to go ahead with his version of Saint Paul's. He used his knowledge of buildings abroad to construct the Cathedral, which he based partly on Saint Peter's Basilica in the Vatican, Italy. It was decorated with beautiful paintings and fine carvings, in a style called 'baroque', which was very grand and was designed to show off wealth and power.

The last of the Stuarts

Charles II's Catholic brother James II succeeded him but was forced to flee abroad. The throne was passed to his daughter Mary, who then ruled jointly with her husband William. He died in 1702, and Mary's sister Anne was on the throne by the time St Paul's Cathedral was finally completed in 1710. When Anne died in 1714 the Stuart line was at an end. During their era the country was changed forever and much of the British monarch's power was handed to Parliament.

GLOSSARY

Bankside The south bank of the River Thames, Tudor London's entertainment district.

Baroque A grand style of architecture and art popular in the 1700s.

Bear-baiting Fights staged between tethered bears and packs of dogs.

Carrack A large wooden ship built in Tudor times.

Catholicism A form of Christian religion with the Pope as head of the Church.

Cavaliers The mounted cavalry of Charles I's Royalist army during the English Civil War.

Civil war A conflict between different forces within a country.

Court Group of nobles and officials who advise the monarch.

Dissolution The destruction of monasteries across England and Wales in 1536, by order of Henry VIII.

Divine right The belief that you are sanctioned by God to do what you like. Tudor and early Stuart monarchs believed they had a divine right to rule how they wished.

Elizabethan During the reign of Elizabeth I from 1533 to 1603.

Great Fire A devastating fire that raged across the City of London in 1666.

Heretic Someone who disagrees with a religion. In Tudor and Stuart times this meant disagreeing with the religion of the ruler.

Jacobean During the reign of James I from 1603 to 1625.

Knot garden A formal garden planted during Elizabethan times, with the plants in geometric patterns.

Monastery A community of monks or nuns.

Musket A long gun first used in the 16th century.

New Model Army The army gathered together by Parliament to oppose King Charles I during the English Civil War.

Parliamentarian Someone who supported the rights of the English Parliament and opposed the Royalists during the English Civil War.

Plague A deadly epidemic that killed a quarter of the population of London in 1665. This outbreak was the last of many such epidemics.

Pottage A vegetable stew eaten by poor people.

Protestantism A form of Christian religion that rejects the Pope as head of the Church.

Puritans A group who held strict Protestant religious beliefs and influenced the policy of Oliver Cromwell, who held power after the English Civil War.

Re-enactor Someone who dresses in authentic historical clothing and re-enacts events in history.

Reformation An era in the 1500s, when the Catholic Church lost power to Protestant rulers in parts of Europe.

Restoration The return of Charles II to the throne in 1660.

Roundhead A nickname for Parliamentarian forces during the English Civil War.

Stuarts The family name of a dynasty who ruled England and Scotland from 1603 to 1714, with a break during the Civil War.

Succession The inheritance of the throne by one family member after another has died.

Tudors The family name of a dynasty who ruled England from 1485 to 1603.

Wattle and daub A type of building style used in medieval and Tudor times, with a wooden frame infilled with woven sticks, mud and dung.

PLACES TO VISIT

Fountains Abbey
Ripon
North Yorkshire
HG4 3DY
www.fountainsabbey.co.uk

The Globe Theatre
21 New Globe Walk
Bankside
London
SE1 9DT
www.shakespeares-globe.org

Hampton Court Palace
East Molesey
Surrey
KT8 9AU
www.hrp.org.uk/Hampton CourtPalace

Llancaiach Fawr Manor
Nelson
Treharris
CF46 6ER
www.caerphilly.gov.uk/llancaiach. fawr

Mary Rose
The Mary Rose Trust,
College Road
HM Naval Base
Portsmouth
PO1 3LX
www.maryrose.org

Montacute House
Montacute
Somerset
TA15 6XP
www.nationaltrust.org.uk/.../w-visits/w-findaplace/w-montacute

Naseby Battlefield
Northamptonshire/Leicestershire border
LE16 9UH
www.battlefieldtrust.com

Pendennis Castle
Cornwall
TR11 4LP
www.english-heritage.org.uk/ server.php?show=nav.11391

Royal Observatory Greenwich
Blackheath Avenue
London
SE10 8XJ
www.nmm.ac.uk

Shakespeare's birthplace and Anne Hathaway's Cottage
Stratford-upon-Avon
Warwickshire

St Mawes Castle
Cornwall
TR2 5DE
www.english-heritage.org. uk/server.php?show=nav.11392

Saint Paul's Cathedral
London
EC4M 8AD
www.stpauls.co.uk

Tower of London
London
EC3N 4AB
www.hrp.org.uk/TowerOfLondon

Weald and Downland Open Air Museum
Singleton
Chichester
West Sussex
PO18 0EU
www.wealddown.co.uk

WEBLINKS
Here are some websites with information about Tudors and Stuarts.
www.bbc.co.uk/history/british/tudors/
www.bbc.co.uk/history/british/civil_war_revolution/
Lots of links and information on Tudor and Stuart eras.

www.spartacus.schoolnet.co.uk/UnitedKingdom.htm
Find out about the personalities of the Tudor and Stuart eras.

www.tudorbritain.org
Run by the Victoria and Albert Museum.
Find out about Tudor life and play online games.

http://english-civil-war-society.org.uk
See photos of English Civil War re-enactments.

Note to parents and teachers
Every effort has been made by the Publishers to ensure that the websites in this book are suitable for children, that they are of the highest educational value, and that they contain no inappropriate or offensive material. However, because of the nature of the Internet, it is impossible to guarantee that the contents of these sites will not be altered. We strongly advise that Internet access is supervised by a responsible adult.

INDEX

Here are the lists of contents for each title in *Tracking Down...*

World War II in Britain
What was World War II? • Running the war • Defending Britain
The battles in the sky • Early warning systems • Air-raid shelters
Life on the Home Front • The children's war • Women in action
The war at sea • The Normandy landings • The end of the war

The Romans in Britain
Romans in Britain • People in Roman Britain • An army base
Busy Londinium • Britain gets roads • Soldier's town • Hadrian's wall
Roman baths and temples • See the show • A country villa
A mystery palace • Enemies from the sea

The Anglo-Saxons in Britain
All about the Anglo-Saxons • Anglo-Saxon people
Last stand of the Brits • Tomb of a king • An ancient church •
Warriors rule • A monk who made history • A Saxon village
A king in hiding • A king's city • One true king • The last battle

The Victorians in Britain
Who were the Victorians? • Queen Victoria at home • Running the country
Industry and manufacturing • The railway age • New ideas and engineering
Beside the seaside • Everyday life • Grand homes for the rich
Children and schools • Victorian health • Crime and punishment

The Vikings in Britain
All about the Vikings • Viking people • Lindisfarne • A great army
A Viking farm • A Viking town • Viking laws • Viking treasure
Shipped to heaven • Viking runes and art • Terror returns • Here to stay

Medieval Life in Britain
All about Medieval Times • Medieval people • The White Tower
Harlech Castle • A manor house • Life as a peasant • Adventurers' Hall
Inside a priory • A cathedral • Medieval art
Going to school • Westminster Abbey

Tudors and Stuarts in Britain
All about Tudor and Stuart Britain • Tudor and Stuart people
Hampton Court palace • Reformation ruins • A dangerous tower
Disaster at sea • A grand house • A trip to the theatre
A busy kitchen • Civil war • A living manor • A monarch's cathedral